SCHIRMER'S LIBRARY
OF MUSICAL CLASSICS

Vol. 1527

Johann Sebastian Bach

Concerto In D Minor

For Piano

Edited by
EDWIN HUGHES

ISBN 0-7935-5226-5

G. SCHIRMER, Inc.

DISTRIBUTED BY

7777 W. BLUEMOUND RD. P.O. BOX 13819 MILWAUKEE, WI 53213

PREFACE

Of the seven concertos by Johann Sebastian Bach for harpsichord and string orchestra, perhaps only one, that in E major, was originally composed for the harpsichord. Three of the others are arrangements of extant concertos for violin, while the remaining three give evidence of a similar origin, although the originals from which they probably sprang have never been located. To this last group belongs the Concerto in D minor, the best known and most frequently performed of any of Bach's compositions in this style. Certain solo passages, notably those in the first movement, with the skipping sixteenth-note figurations circling around long, open-string organ-points, indicate rather conclusively its origin as a work for a bowed instrument.

As the most prolific arranger among all the great composers of his own and others' works, with the exception of Liszt, Bach did not fail to utilize the D minor Concerto still further. The first movement is found turned to good account as the instrumental introduction to the cantata, "Wir müssen durch viel Trübsal in das Reich Gottes eingehen," while the slow movement forms the basis of the principal chorus in the same cantata. The power and the compelling rhythmic swing of the first movement and the depth and appealing fervor of the chaconne-like Adagio were evidently potent enough in the mind of the composer to warrant their appearing in more than one setting.

In his later years, Bach collected his harpsichord concertos and gave them the finishing touches. The manuscripts of the scores are in the National Library in Berlin, but authentic reprints are available in the Bach Gesellschaft Edition, which has been taken as the basis for the text of the present edition of the D minor Concerto.

As with all of Bach's compositions, marks of interpretation in the original are largely notable through their absence. The tempo captions of the three movements, however, are from the composer's hand, as is the indication, "Adagio," just before the final tutti in the last movement. There is not a single original dynamic sign in the solo part from start to finish, unless one regard as such the pointed staccato dots found in the first movement, which may be taken to indicate sharply accented staccati.

With the exception of an occasional short slur, there are no signs of phrasing given in the first and last movements. In this respect the Adagio is somewhat better off, although the articulation is far more in the character of that of a bowed than of a keyboard instrument. These marks, together with the alternating "forte" and "piano" which are found at intervals in the tutti passages, have been retained in the present edition. All remaining signs of interpretation, including indications of tempo change within the movements, dynamics, touch, phrasing, and, of course, pedalling and metronome marks, are suggestions on the part of the present editor to those who have not already formed their own conclusions as to these matters. While it is hoped that they will be found useful, they do not seek to inhibit further experiments in the direction of a styleful conception and a musical interpretation of the work.

The solo instrument in Bach's concertos is a glorified obbligato to the whole rather than the brilliant display of instrumental prowess, set off against a colorful orchestral background, to which we are accustomed in modern works for piano and orchestra. In Bach's day the soloist in a harpsichord concerto sat in the midst of a small group of strings, from a dozen to perhaps eighteen, with the leader of the orchestra presiding at a second harpsichord and filling in at the tutti with an accompaniment improvised from the figured bass or "continuo." To modern ears the string parts are quite sufficient unto themselves, and a second keyboard instrument in the ensemble would hardly be a welcome addition. The soloist had no long-continued measures of rests to count when the orchestra entered, but played his part in the tutti passages along with the other executants. In the present edition, a too-insistent solo instrument has been avoided by leaving the long tutti entirely to the strings.

The editor is not of the opinion that the D minor Concerto or any other of Bach's works for harpsichord and orchestra, for that matter, suffers to any undue degree in its musical beauty and effectiveness by being performed on the modern pianoforte instead of on the harpsichord. However, it is important to bear in mind that there are certain very important differences in the expressive possibilities of the two instruments from a dynamic standpoint.

Abrupt changes of tone quality and quantity were the only means of dynamic expression at the command of the harpsichordist (hence the frequent alternation of the indications, "forte" and "piano," in Bach's harpsichord compositions, such as the Goldberg Variations), for it was impossible from the nature of the instrument to shade a passage or a melody from note to note. By means of stops, similar to those on the organ, however, octave couplings and the coupling of the manuals were possible. This arrangement, together with alternation in the use of the quill and leather plectra and of the hands on the two manuals, placed at the disposal of the player a tonal palette of much variety, although a crescendo or decrescendo as we know it on the piano was entirely out of the question.

It is impossible to believe that Bach would not have made use of the crescendo and decrescendo if he had had a concert instrument capable of executing them, and it would be the purest pedantry to avoid their use to-day, even in those works of the Master which were written indisputably for performance on the harpsichord. The abrupt changes from piano to forte and vice versa are equally at the disposal of the pianist as the harpsichordist, and, in addition, the command over a wealth of dynamic nuance quite out of the reach of performers on the older instrument. The dynamic indications in the present edition are based on these considerations.

The harpsichords of Bach's day possessed no damper pedal, but there is no reason why present-day performers should return to tonal dryness after that very important mechanical adjunct has been in the meantime added to the musical resources of keyboard instruments. In this edition of the D minor Concerto, pedal indications will be found throughout the solo part, not in the manner of modern "pedal effects," however, nor in an overabundance which would rob the performance of that clarity of outline which is one of the chief charms of the harpsichord.

With regard to the fingering, it should be noted that, in those places where the two hands are written on one staff, the figures above the notes indicate the use of the right hand, those below, of the left.

EDWIN HUGHES.

34028

Concerto
in D minor

Edited by Edwin Hughes

Johann Sebastian Bach

Piano I

Piano II
(String Orchestra)

I

I

* The solo instrument may omit the opening six measures upon performing with orchestra.

34028

Tutti

Solo

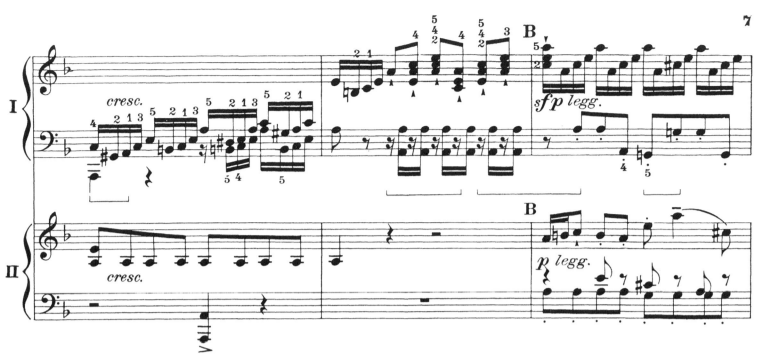

Ped. simile

34028

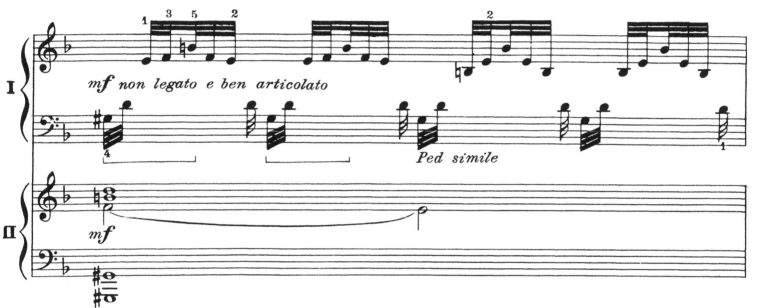

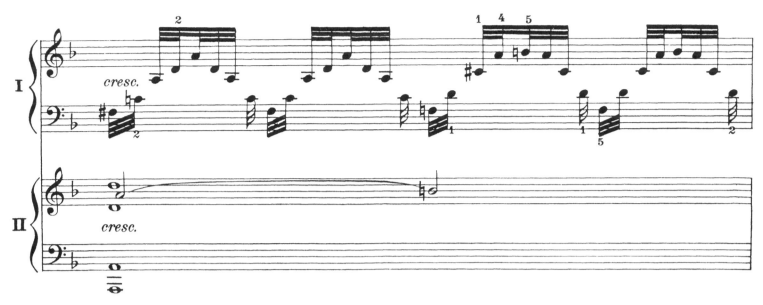

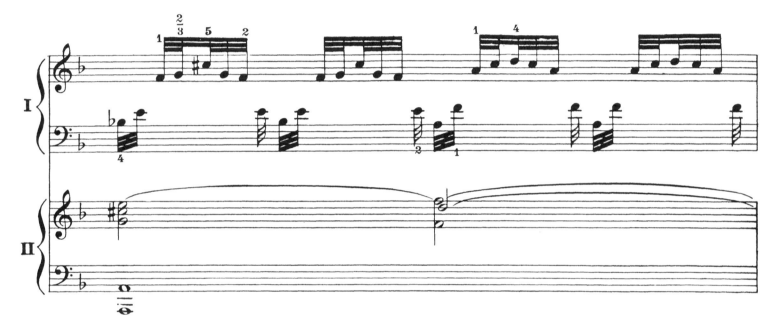

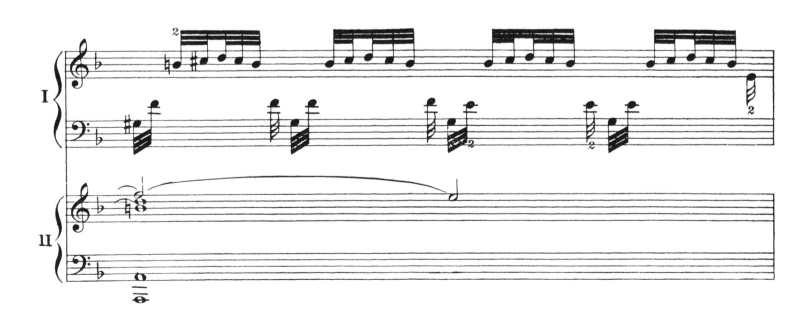

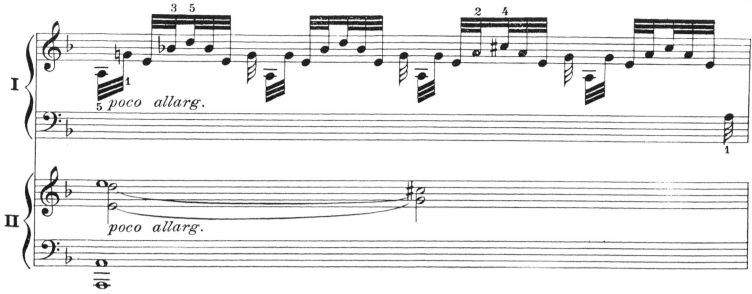

* For a more concise close to the movement, the following twelve measures may be omitted.

34028

Ped.simile

34028

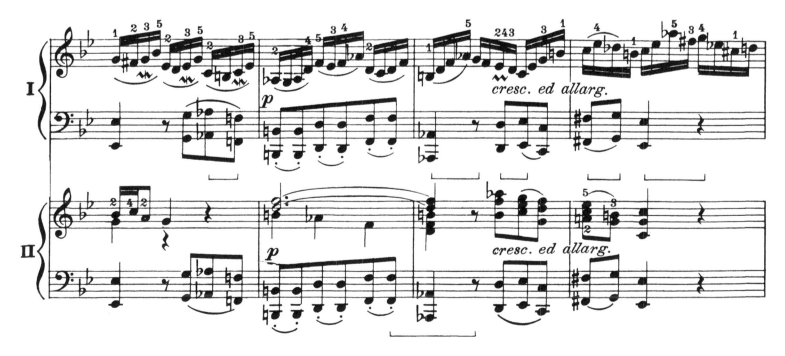

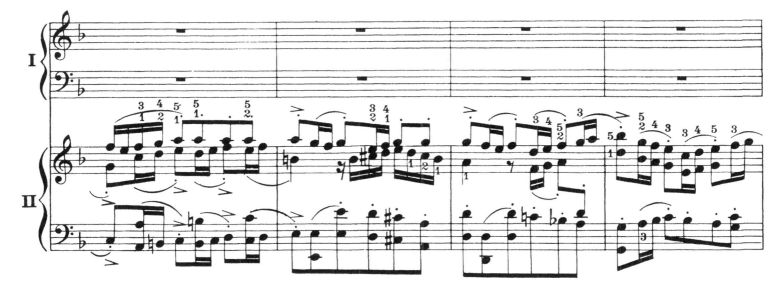

84028

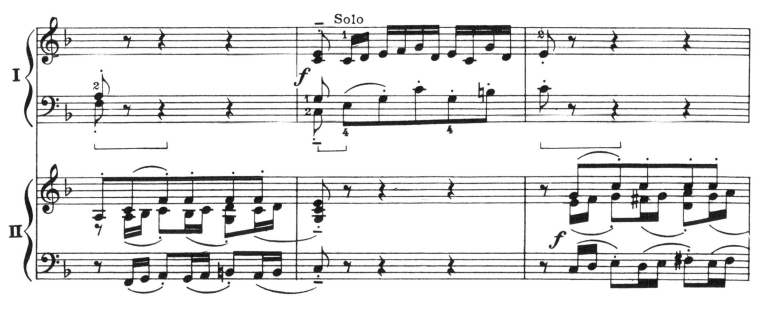

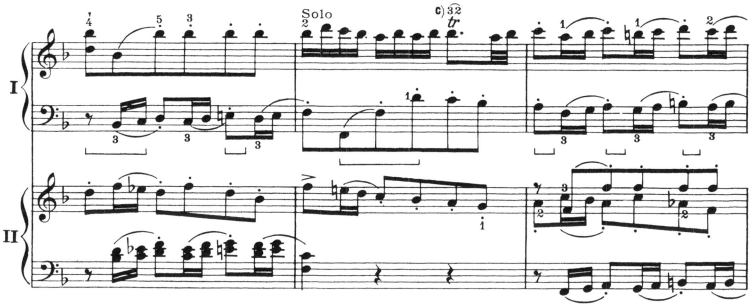

d)

*) For those who find the last movement growing slightly prolix toward the end, a cut of 19 measures (to the next ✻)
may be recommended.

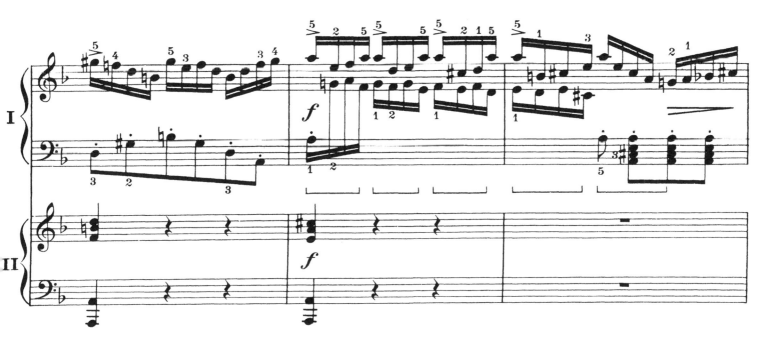

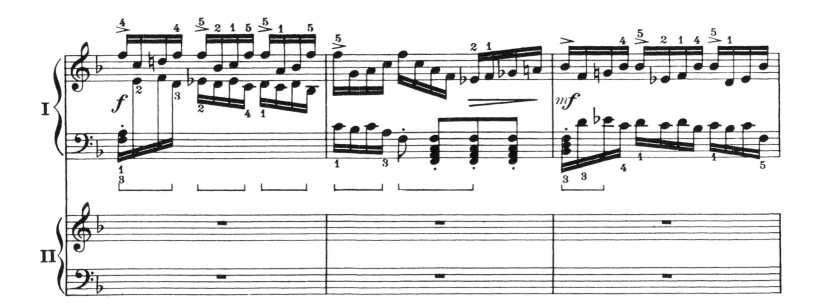

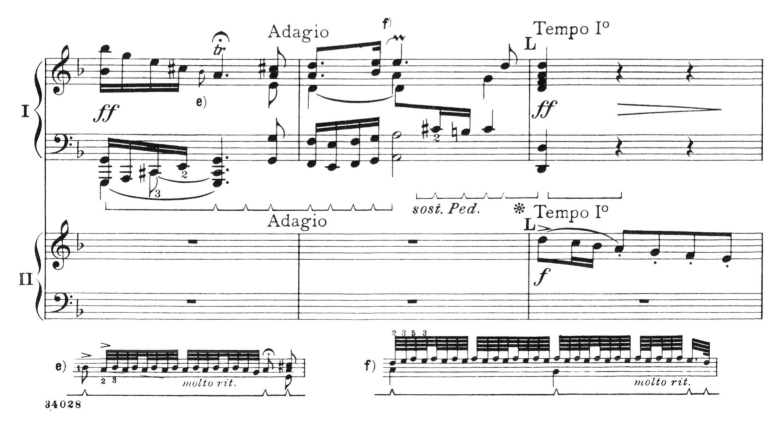